THE
MARMITE®
WORLD
COOKBOOK

THE MARMITE

WORLD COOKBOOK

by Paul Hartley

A.

First published in Great Britain
in 2010
by **Absolute Press**
Scarborough House
29 James Street West
Bath BA1 2BT England
Phone 44 (0) 1225 316013
Fax 44 (0) 1225 445836
E-mail info@absolutepress.co.uk
Web www.absolutepress.co.uk

Publisher
Jon Croft
Commissioning Editor
Meg Avent
Art Direction
Matt Inwood
Design
Matt Inwood and
Claire Siggery
Photography
Mike Cooper
Food Stylist
Genevieve Taylor

A catalogue record of this book
is available from the British Library.

ISBN 9781906650360

Printed and bound in Slovenia on
behalf of Latitude Press.

**Picture credits (some of which
have been digitally enhanced)**
old photo 1 © Jumpingsack used
as background image throughout;
empty international airport
departures board © nmcandre
(pages 67-68); sky with clouds
© João Freitas (pages 32); swarm
of mosquitos © AlienCat (page 32);
Hawaiian lei made of orchid blooms
© Christopher Howey (page 32);
airplane © MC_PP (page 31);
taj mahal © hugy (pages 7,57);
card for greeting or congratulation
on the blue floral background
© Loraliu (page 6); ancient map
of the world © javarman (page 11
and others); the great pyramids of
Giza © Mark Physsas (pages 7,43);
Eiffel Tower © Richard McGuirk
(pages 7,11); Stonehenge © Kpics
(page 72); Sydney Opera House
and Harbour Bridge © Chee-Onn
Leong (page 52); photo de New
York © dje2303 (page 28); Maya
pyramid © Alex Garaev (page 18);
torn taper with masking tape
© robynmac (page 11 and others);
planet Earth © Dan Marsh (front
cover, page 79 and others); Leaning
Tower of Pisa © Helen Shorey
(page 63); horizon © Papo (page 47).

Contents

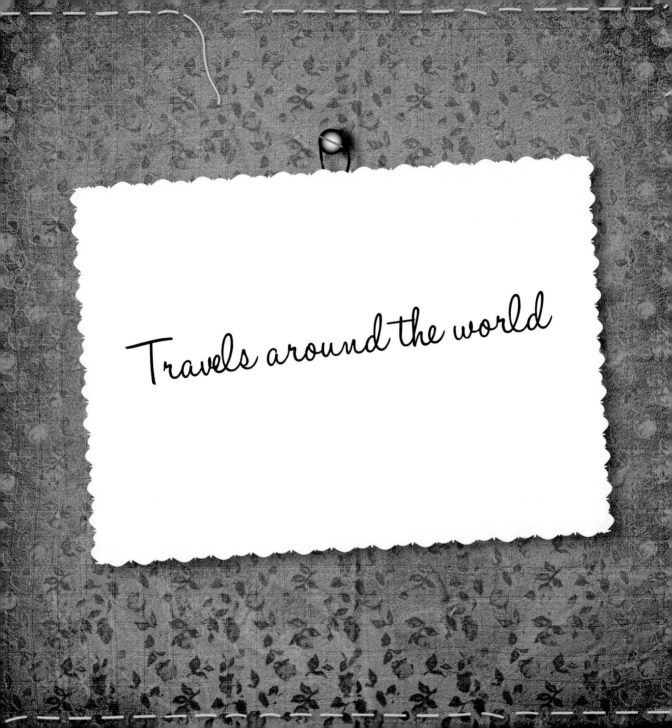

For many, Marmite has become one of those essentials in life. A daily constant that we can't live without. Marmite has travelled the world in countless suitcases and travel bags, through export markets galore and even, so legend has it, via the British Embassy's 'diplomatic bag'.

Through accident, experiment and outright wilful hedonism, Marmite has managed to infiltrate its salty elixir into some of the finest and most far-flung cuisines of the world... slowly mingling into the tagines of North Africa, dressing thin, buttery strips of Italian pasta, bashing the edges of the Great British roast potato. What follows is a selection of recipes from around the world where a little Marmite magic has lifted very good dishes to new-found heights. Go yeast, go west, go all around the world via this rather wonderful recipe collection....

Crispy Coated Salmon Goujons with Homemade Tartare Sauce

Fish and chips is a British institution and served with tartare sauce becomes one of the finest dishes in the world. It's sad then that it is so often wrecked with manufactured goujons and uninteresting tartare sauce. This recipe is the real deal though, and enhancing it with Marmite makes this classic a winner the world over.

SERVES 4

For the tartare sauce
4 tablespoons mayonnaise
2 teaspoons capers, rinsed and finely chopped
2 small gherkins, finely chopped
1 spring onion, finely chopped
salt and pepper

800g salmon fillet
1 tablespoon Marmite, warmed
100g flour seasoned with a good pinch of dried herbs
2 free-range eggs, beaten
100g fresh white breadcrumbs
sunflower oil, for deep-frying

Put all the tartare sauce ingredients into a small bowl and mix together. Season lightly with salt and pepper.

Take the salmon fillet and slice it into goujons about 10cm long and 1.5cm wide. Now for the messy bit! Brush each of the goujons lightly all over with the Marmite and lay out in a shallow dish. You will need three more shallow dishes – one for the seasoned flour, one for the beaten egg and one for the breadcrumbs.

Heat the oil to 190C or when a small cube of bread sizzles when dropped in. Now roll each goujon in flour, then in the egg and finally roll it in the breadcrumbs. You can do this in batches and fry for 3–4 minutes a batch or until crispy and golden. Keep each batch warm on kitchen paper on a baking tray in the oven. Repeat until all the goujons are cooked.

Serve your scrummy goujons with a crispy leaf salad, wedges of lemon and your own tartare sauce – it's that simple.

Crudités with Marmite Peanut Dip

Inspired by a Sri Lankan chef and recreated by me, this will seriously have your taste buds bouncing with excitement. Crudités are the perfect starter for a supper with friends.

SERVES 6–8

For the dip
250g crunchy peanut butter
2 garlic cloves, crushed
2.5cm fresh ginger, finely chopped
juice of 1 lemon
1 tablespoon light soy sauce
1 tablespoon Marmite
2 tablespoons runny honey
1 teaspoon ground turmeric
dash of Tabasco sauce
150ml water

For the crudités
1 small fresh cauliflower
2 large carrots
1 red pepper
1 yellow pepper
4 stalks of celery
1 bunch radishes

First, make the dip by putting all the ingredients into a blender. Blitz until you have a smooth dipping sauce. If it seems a little too thick, add a dash more water. Put the dip into a suitable bowl and cover with clingfilm until you are ready to serve.

Cut the cauliflower into bite-sized florets, peel the carrots and cut them into sticks about 8cm long. Halve and deseed the peppers trimming off any pith inside and cut them lengthways into the same-sized strips. Wash the celery stalks thoroughly and then run a potato peeler down the outside curve of each stalk to remove any stringy bits and cut to the same size as the peppers and carrots. Top and tail the radishes and wash well.

Using a large plate, put the dip bowl in the centre and arrange the carrots, peppers and celery neatly around it. Add the cauliflower florets around the sticks and strips, and finally the radishes around the cauliflower and you are ready to serve.

Marmite Rocket Pocket

This brunch pocket is packed with goodness and flavour, really easy to prepare and won't cost your pocket a packet. The savoury splendour of the bacon and Marmite sits so well alongside the gorgeous flavours of oozing French Brie and peppery rocket.

PER PERSON

3 rashers streaky bacon
50g ripe Brie
1 large tomato
1 handful of rocket leaves
balsamic vinegar
olive oil
1 pitta bread
Marmite, for spreading

Grill the rashers of streaky bacon until crispy, then dice. Chop up the Brie and tomato and put them in a bowl with the bacon, a good handful of rocket leaves, a dash of balsamic vinegar and drizzle with a little olive oil. Mix everything together well.

Take the pitta bread and cut a crescent off along the long edge, pop into a toaster open side down for only a minute to open up the bread. Now, carefully open up the pitta and spread a generous amount of Marmite inside and pack in the rocket, tomato, Brie and bacon. Serve deliciously warm for a perfect brunch.

Quick check in
Oui, oui! It's the self-styled gastronomical, cultural and romantic capital of the world.

Departure lounge
They gave us Brits and the rest of the world the 'other' option on our hotel morning menus: the Continental breakfast.

Customs clearance
The French like to do some things formally and some with a touch more intimacy. Brush up on when to shake hands and when to plant a smacker or two on the cheeks.

Nothing (else) to declare?
The original *bon viveurs*, the French love their food and love their wine and love to love. And they love excess. What's not to love?

On the culinary map
From croque-monsieurs to croissants, and coffee to coq-au-vin, there's much to admire about the French way with food.

Off the radar
Frogs' legs and snails – so goes the cultural cliché – though not many French enjoy these dishes either.

Chicken Caesar Salad with Marmite Croûtons

Italian restaurateur Caesar Cardini is believed to have created this classic and much-loved salad one night in his restaurant by using ingredients that were to hand. They say you can't top perfection, but with the addition of Marmite, I would beg to differ!

SERVES 4

For the Caesar dressing
2 free-range eggs
1 clove of garlic
4 anchovy fillets
1 tablespoon lemon juice
1 tablespoon white wine vinegar
1 teaspoon capers, rinsed
freshly ground black pepper
150ml olive oil

2 Romaine or Cos lettuces
small bag mixed leaves
2 chicken breasts, poached in
 chicken stock and cooled
2 tablespoons olive oil
2 teaspoons Marmite
4 slices stale bread, diced into
 small cubes
1 teaspoon dried mixed herbs

To make the Caesar dressing place the eggs into boiling water and leave for only 2 minutes, then plunge them straight into cold water. Next, break the eggs into a blender: the yolk should drop in easily and the whites will need to be scraped from the shells with a teaspoon. Now add all the other ingredients except the olive oil. Switch on the blender and gradually add the olive oil until you have a rich creamy dressing. Leftover dressing will keep in a sealed jar in the fridge for up to a week.

Cut the base off the lettuces and pull the leaves apart, discarding any that are not perfect and wash and dry them on a clean tea towel. Select 16 of the nicest leaves and arrange them like petals in 4 pasta bowls or similar dishes. Roughly chop the remaining leaves, combine them with the mixed leaves and toss them in a bowl with the Caesar salad dressing. Drizzle a little of the salad dressing over the Cos or Romaine leaves around the 4 serving bowls.

Pile the mixed salad into the centre of each bowl. Slice the chicken breasts as thinly as possible lengthways and arrange them on top of the salad, also in the shape of petals so that you have a mound in the centre.

Warm the olive oil in a frying pan over a medium heat and stir in the Marmite. When it is mixed, add the bread cubes and sprinkle over the dried herbs then keep the bread moving in the pan until you have hot crispy croutons. Tip them out onto kitchen paper to soak up any excess oil and scatter over the chicken.

Spicy Mushroom and Black Bean Tacos with Onions and Cheese

Those Mexicans have an incredible ability to make your mouth water just at the thought of a warm filled taco. This is my interpretation of an authentic recipe – but one not for the faint-hearted! A medley of wonderful flavours fuse together and make devouring this a total joy!

MAKES 12 TACOS

For the pasillo paste
8 garlic cloves, unpeeled
4 hot red chillies, cut lengthways and deseeded
1 teaspoon dried oregano
$\frac{1}{4}$ teaspoon freshly ground black pepper
$\frac{1}{4}$ teaspoon ground cumin

1 tablespoon olive oil
2 teaspoons Marmite
120ml water
200g tinned black beans, drained
200g mixed wild mushrooms, broken into smaller pieces
2 tablespoons freshly chopped coriander
12 corn tortillas
1 small onion, finely diced
25g dry feta cheese, crumbled

You can make the pasillo paste a few days ahead and refrigerate

First make the pasillo paste by placing the garlic cloves on a dry griddle or heavy based frying pan over a medium heat. After about 10 minutes the insides should be soft and the outside blackening. While this is roasting, add the chillies to the pan and press them down with a spatula for a few minutes on each side to toast. Peel or squeeze out the garlic into a blender, add the chillies, oregano, pepper, cumin and about 100ml water so that you can blitz it all into a paste.

Heat the oil in a heavy-based saucepan or deep-sided frying pan and carefully add the pasillo. Stir for 5 minutes until all the delicious spices concentrate and the mixture thickens then add the Marmite, water, black beans, mushrooms and coriander, reserving a little to garnish. Simmer for about 15 minutes, stirring occasionally, until the mushrooms are soft and the sauce has reduced. Taste and season if required

If you have a vegetable steamer wrap the tortillas in a clean tea towel, place them inside the steamer and boil the water for one minute. Remove from the heat and do not open the steamer. Leave for 15 minutes. (Alternatively, you can warm them in a gentle oven wrapped in foil.)

Tip the mushrooms into a warm serving dish, scatter with the onions, cheese and remaining coriander and serve with a basket of your warm tortillas for your guests to assemble their tacos.

Marmite Bloody Mary

It was Mary Queen of Scots who supposedly gave her name to the 'Bloody Mary' and I don't doubt that she would have lost her head for this one! I've taken out the Worcestershire sauce and replaced it with Marmite to give it a sensational new twist.

PER PERSON

1 level teaspoon Marmite
couple of dashes of Tabasco
   sauce
1 tablespoon lemon juice
pinch of white pepper
25ml vodka
100ml tomato juice
celery salt
1 stick of celery

In a jug mix together the Marmite, Tabasco, lemon juice and pepper. Add the vodka and tomato juice and whisk it all together – a cocktail shaker looks more flamboyant and will produce a more textured drink.

Fill a tall glass halfway with ice and pour the mixture over the ice. Sprinkle with a little celery salt and serve with a stick of celery.

Marmite-Glazed Lamb Shanks with Crushed Cannellini Beans

This is a wonderful piece of British comfort food – one that can virtually cook itself once you've done a bit of preparation. The aroma that wafts from the oven will have your taste buds tingling in anticipation. Perfect to share with friends around a log fire on cold winter nights.

SERVES 4

For the lamb shanks
4 lamb shanks
200ml white wine
3 tablespoons redcurrant jelly
1 tablespoon Marmite
1 tablespoon Worcestershire
   sauce
2 large cloves garlic, finely diced
4 tablespoons olive oil
8 shallots, roughly chopped
few sprigs fresh thyme

25g butter
1 leek, trimmed and shredded
1 teaspoon Dijon mustard
2 x 400g tins cannellini beans
salt and black pepper
1 tablespoon chopped flatleaf
   parsley
olive oil

Put all the ingredients for the lamb shanks into a large freezer bag, squidge the whole lot together and pop them in the fridge to marinate overnight.

Preheat the oven to 220C/425F/Gas 7. Empty the lamb shanks and all of their juices into a roasting tin and pop this into the centre of the oven turning it down straight away to 160C/325F/Gas 3. Roast for 2 hours so that the meat just falls away tenderly from the bones.

In a frying pan melt the butter and add the shredded leeks. Fry for 2–3 minutes until softened, stir in the mustard and then add the cannellini beans. Season with salt and pepper, scatter with parsley and then cook, stirring, for 2–3 minutes until the beans are thoroughly heated through. Using the back of a fork, lightly crush the cannellini beans and then drizzle with a little olive oil.

Place the beans onto serving plates, lay the lamb shanks on top and then drizzle a little of the roasting juices over them – perfect!

Quick check-in
Mexico: home of the Aztec ruins, the sombrero, the bandit moustache and an eponymous capital city.

Departure lounge
Mexico gave the world tequila and with it one of the worst hangovers known to man.

Customs clearance
When eating out, waiters are referred to as *joven* (young man) – regardless of their age.

Nothing (else) to declare?
Mexican pace is slow and laid back and so to arrive half an hour late is not considered rude.

On the culinary map
A big *muchas gracias* from the rest of the world for such wonders as guacamole, burritos, enchiladas and nachos.

Off the radar
The home of the chilli pepper. Make sure you're at the right end of the Scoville scale and with a glass of water to hand!

Georgian Feast Bread

This bread is known as *Khachapuri* and is sold as warm buns by street vendors in Georgia. You can use any cheese – the Georgians will often use goat's cheese – but this is my favourite combination.

MAKES 4 BUNS

1 x 7g sachet easy-blend yeast
150ml warm milk
225g strong white bread flour
1 teaspoon salt
25g unsalted butter, softened
1 egg yolk

For the filling
200g mature Cheddar cheese, grated
200g ricotta cheese
1 egg, beaten
1 tablespoon softened butter
freshly ground black pepper
4 teaspoons Marmite

You will need a greased Yorkshire pudding tin with 4 x 10cm holes.

Mix together the yeast and warm milk and leave to stand for 5 minutes until it becomes foamy. Sieve the flour and salt into a large bowl, add the yeast liquid and mix to a dough. Knead in the softened butter and then turn it out onto a lightly-floured surface. Knead the dough for at least 5 minutes or until it is a smooth and elastic dough. Put the dough into a lightly-oiled bowl, cover with clingfilm and leave in a warm place for up to 1$\frac{1}{2}$ hours or until it has risen and doubled in size.

In a bowl mix together the cheeses, egg and softened butter and season with plenty of pepper.

Turn out the dough onto a floured surface and knead again for 3 minutes then divide it into 4. Roll each piece out to a 20cm circle and carefully lay one in the hole of the baking tin. Drop in one teaspoon of Marmite and then add some of the cheese mixture. Gather up the overhanging dough and pinch it together and twist it to make a topknot. Repeat with the other 3 dough rings. Cover with a clean tea towel and leave to rise in a warm place for 25–30 minutes.

Preheat the oven to 108C/350F/ Gas 4. Mix the egg yolk with a splash of water and brush all over the dough then bake for 25–30 minutes until golden. Leave in the tin to cool a little and then serve warm so that the melted cheese and Marmite in the centre will ooze out when the bread is broken.

Jamaican Curried Goat

Curried goat is eaten the world over, but mainly in the Caribbean where it is almost a national dish. This is strong in texture, strong in spices and strong in flavour – if you like curry you'll just love this.

SERVES 6

For the Jamaican curry powder
1 tablespoon coriander seeds
1 tablespoon black peppercorns
12 whole green cardamom pods
1 teaspoon fenugreek seeds
10cm cinnamon stick, broken into
   pieces
1 teaspoon ground ginger
1 teaspoon ground turmeric
1 teaspoon ground allspice

2 tablespoons vegetable oil
1 large onion, chopped
2 cloves garlic, finely chopped
2 medium-sized hot red chillies,
   deseeded and finely diced
100g Jamaican curry powder
1kg goat meat, cubed
1 tablespoon fresh thyme leaves
2 tablespoons Marmite

First, create your curry powder. This recipe will make a batch for future if you store it in an airtight jar – and you will definitely want to use it again, especially with lamb curries.

Put all the curry spices into a herb grinder or coffee grinder (or crush with pestle and mortar) and blitz until you have a coarse powder. Measure out 100g and store the rest.

Heat the oil in a large heavy-based saucepan or flameproof casserole. Fry the onions until soft then add the garlic, chillies and a quarter of the curry powder. Add the meat and brown it gently, keeping it moving all the time so that it doesn't catch on the pan and burn. Once the juices start to run add the remaining curry powder, the thyme leaves, Marmite and enough water to just cover the meat.

Cover the pan, reduce the heat to low and simmer for $1\frac{1}{2}$ hours, checking every so often that it is not too dry. You may need to add a little more water as it cooks. When the curry is cooked and the goat meat is tender you can thicken it traditionally with fresh breadcrumbs if you wish, or leave a thinner gravy for dunking.

WHOLE LOTTA LOAF GOIN' ON

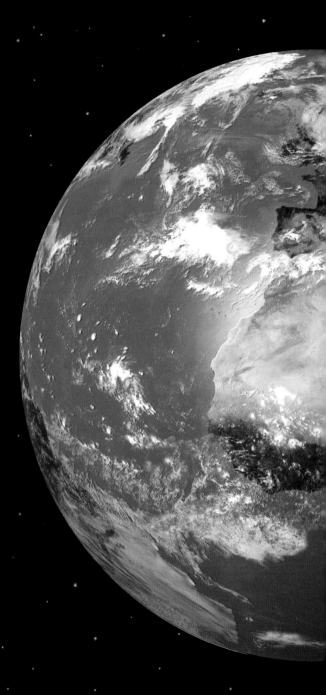

The world's most widely eaten food?

That would have to be bread, the staff of life and a staple in the diets of people from all over the world dating back to the early days of mankind.

Across Britain, Europe and North America, yeast-based breads are the most popular. Throughout the rest of the world there are many other varieties of bread; many are types of flatbread which don't use leavening agents and many are made from batter or kneaded dough. Bread can be baked, fried or steamed.

From bagels to baguettes, chapatis to ciabattas, pittas to parathas, matzo to muffins, to name but just a few, bread would seem to be the one staple we just cannot live without!

BEST TAKEN WITH A PINCH OF SALT...

...and a dash of chilli sauce... and a shot of something strong. Indeed, anything that might help disguise these top five unpalatable foods from around the world!

1. Fugu
Fugu is the poisonous puffer fish from Japan, containing enough poison to be lethal. Only trained chefs can prepare it for consumption and only the brave dare eat it!

2. Casu Marzu
Meaning literally 'rotten cheese', this pungent sheep's milk cheese from Sardinia contains live insect larvae. It can be 'enjoyed' with or without the larvae.

3. Hákarl
Fermented shark is widely available in Iceland. The shark meat is fermented for two to four months. The strong ammonia smell is said to be far worse than the taste.

4. Sannakji
In Korea, small live octopus are sliced up and seasoned with sesame oil. With tentacles still wriggling when served, you must take care not to let the suction cups stick to your throat!

5. Haggis
The classic Scottish dish made from the minced liver, lung and heart of a sheep, mixed with onion, oats, spices and seasoning and all boiled up in the sheep's stomach. Yum!

Marmite and Chilli-Glazed Carrots with Honey and Orange

If you've never cooked roast vegetables infused with Marmite then you have missed out, it adds huge amounts to the final flavour. In this recipe I have converted plain vegetables into a delicious dish.

SERVES 6–8 AS AN ACCOMPANIMENT

30g unsalted butter
1 tablespoon olive oil
2 teaspoons Marmite
8 medium carrots, peeled and
  thickly sliced
1 tablespoon runny honey
1 small red chilli, deseeded and
  finely diced
1 tablespoon balsamic vinegar
juice of $\frac{1}{2}$ orange
fresh thyme leaves to garnish

Preheat the oven to 180C/350F/ Gas 4.

Place the butter and oil in a roasting tin and pop it into the oven for 5 minutes. Remove it and stir in the Marmite. Now add the carrots and the remaining ingredients except the thyme and mix them all well to completely combine the lovely flavours.

Roast in the oven for 25–30 minutes until cooked through and just golden. Remove with a slotted spoon to a warm serving dish and scatter the thyme leaves over the top.

Marmite Yorkies with Beef and Rosemary

A miniature spin on a British classic. This is perfect party food which looks good and tastes great.

MAKES 12 FILLED YORKIES

12 frozen mini Yorkshire puddings, defrosted
4 teaspoons Marmite
6 slices rare roast beef (perfect if you have leftovers)
2 tablespoons mayonnaise mixed with 1 teaspoon ready-made hot horseradish sauce
12 mini sprigs of fresh rosemary

Preheat the oven to 200C/400F/Gas 6

Place the Yorkshire puddings in a roasting tin and drop about one third of a teaspoon of Marmite into the bottom of each one. Then, using the back of a teaspoon, gently spread it over the base. Pop them into the oven and cook for 5–8 minutes until crispy.

Arrange the Yorkshire puddings on a serving dish and crumple half a slice of beef into each one so that it stands up in the pudding. Add a little dollop of horseradish mayonnaise to each and finish with a sprig of rosemary.

Hearty Lamb and Chickpea Soup

There are many variations on this comforting soup from Libya, but to my mind the addition of Marmite adds an extra richness that really works.

SERVES 4

1 tablespoon vegetable oil
1 large onion, finely chopped
2 celery stalks, finely chopped
1 clove garlic, crushed
1 teaspoon grated fresh ginger
$\frac{1}{2}$ teaspoon ground cinnamon
$\frac{1}{4}$ teaspoon ground nutmeg
freshly ground black pepper
250g diced shoulder of lamb
1 x 400g tin chopped tomatoes
1 tablespoon Marmite mixed with
1 litre hot water
1 x 400g tin chickpeas, drained
    and rinsed
200g tinned red lentils, drained
    and rinsed
1 tablespoon lemon juice
handful fresh coriander leaves,
    roughly chopped

Heat the oil in a large saucepan or flameproof casserole dish and add the onion, celery, garlic and ginger and cook stirring until the onion softens. Next add the cinnamon, nutmeg and plenty of black pepper and cook for a few more minutes until fragrant. Add the lamb and cook for 5 minutes, turning it until browned.

Now add the tomatoes and Marmite stock, cover and cook for 1 hour on a gentle simmer. Next, tip in the chickpeas and lentils, stir to mix in and simmer for a further 30 minutes or until you have a thick rich soup.

When you are ready to serve, stir in the lemon juice and coriander leaves and enjoy.

Moroccan Chicken Tagine with Prunes and Almonds

A tagine, for those who don't know, is a pot that consists of two parts: a cone-shaped lid that sits on a large round dish base. As food cooks, the flavours steam upwards through the food producing a gorgeous fragrant Moroccan aroma.

SERVES 4

2 teaspoons cumin seeds
2 teaspoons ground coriander
1 teaspoon smoked paprika
2 teaspoons ground cumin
1 x 10cm cinnamon stick
2 tablespoons olive oil
2 teaspoons Marmite
10 chicken thighs, skinned, boned and cubed
2 large onions, diced
2 cloves garlic, crushed
500ml chicken stock
250ml glass red wine
100g ready-to-eat stoned prunes
40g flaked almonds
1 teaspoon caster sugar
$1/2$ teaspoon salt
1 tablespoon chopped flat-leaf parsley

Dry-fry the cumin seeds until fragrant, then add in the coriander, paprika, ground cumin and cinnamon stick. Stir and remove from the heat.

Heat the oil and Marmite in a tagine or large heavy-based saucepan. Add the chicken and fry until coated and sealed. Take off the heat and remove the chicken with a slotted spoon, reserving the oil and juices and set aside.

Now add the onions and garlic to the existing oil in the tagine or saucepan and fry for 5 minutes until the onion softens. Return the chicken to the pan together with the dry-fried spices, the stock and the wine. Bring to the boil, then cover and simmer for 45 minutes.

Stir in the prunes and cook uncovered for a further 15 minutes

Heat a small, dry frying pan and add in the flaked almonds, then the sugar and salt, and keep them moving around the pan until the almonds turn golden at the edges. Tip them out onto kitchen paper and as they cool they will crispen.

Serve the chicken tagine in bowls scattered with the salty, sugary almonds and parsley.

Quick check-in
Home to Hollywood, the hamburger, the stars and stripes, Elvis and the good ol' American Dream.

Departure lounge
If America has given anything to the world of food, it's fast food. America did it faster first and franchised it out before anyone else.

Customs clearance
Everything is that little bit bigger and easier to get at in the US – the land of the SuperSize and the 7/11 and where everything is available 24/7.

Nothing (else) to declare?
America's most famous food staples are borrowed and improved on from all over the world – the German burger, the Italian pizza, English apple pie. It's the world's melting pot of all other cuisines.

On the culinary map
Pecan pie is as indigenously and deliciously American as it gets.
Try gumbo too: a wonderful, warming Louisiana stew.

Off the radar
You might wish to pass on chitterlings – the boiled or stewed small intestines of a pig. And maybe hog's head stew too.

Travels around the world
NO.3 America

Spinach, Marmite and Cottage Cheese Filo Parcels

This is a really scrummy Greek-influenced dish, perfect for vegetarians, fun to make and fun to serve.

MAKES 12 PARCELS

250g fresh baby leaf spinach, washed
2 teaspoons Marmite
freshly ground black pepper
250g cottage cheese
50g melted butter
1 pack ready-made filo pastry, defrosted if frozen
12 chive stems

You will also need a pastry brush and a clean damp tea towel

First, prepare the spinach by boiling a little water in a saucepan. Add the spinach and turn it a few times in the water until it has just wilted. Drain and when just cool enough to handle, squeeze out as much excess water as possible. Put into a small bowl and stir in the Marmite until it is well mixed then season with pepper.

Preheat the oven to 180C/350F/ Gas 4. With your spinach, cottage cheese and melted butter to hand you can now prepare the filo pastry. You will need to work fairly quickly and carefully with the pastry to avoid it drying out, but it's well worth the effort. Unroll the pastry sheets and lay out on a clean surface, covered with the damp tea towel.

Take one sheet of pastry and paint it all over with melted butter, then repeat with 2 more sheets all on top of each other. Cut out 4 squares (roughly 12cm in length, with each square being 3 filo sheets deep) and discard any leftovers. Into the centre of each square put a heaped teaspoon of spinach and a heaped teaspoon of cottage cheese. Now pick up the 4 corners of a pastry square and pinch together, twisting slightly to form a little sealed parcel. Place on a greased baking sheet and brush with a little more melted butter. Repeat with 2 more triple-thick filo sheets until you have made 12 parcels.

Bake in the centre of the oven for 8–10 minutes until just golden and crispy. When cooled a little, tie a stem of chive around the neck of each parcel to serve.

Baked Stuffed Globe Artichokes

The basis of this dish hails from Andalucia in Spain where I believe the best artichokes grow. These stuffed artichokes will make any dinner party a huge success – it's a very impressive dish, packed with flavour.

SERVES 2

4 shallots, finely diced
1 clove garlic, finely diced
1 tablespoon olive oil
$\frac{1}{2}$ red pepper, diced
250g minced beef
1 tablespoon tomato purée
2 teaspoons Marmite
1 teaspoon dried mixed herbs
freshly ground black pepper
400ml water
50g chorizo, rind removed and
  diced
juice of $\frac{1}{2}$ lemon
2 globe artichokes
40g grated Cheddar cheese

You will need a large pan, large enough to sit the artichokes in side by side

Fry the shallots and garlic in the oil until soft and then add the pepper and cook for 3 minutes. Next add the minced beef and break it up with a fork until it is separated and browned and follow with the purée, Marmite, herbs, a good grind of black pepper and the water. Simmer for one hour or until you have a thick rich meaty sauce with very little juice. Stir in the chorizo.

To a large pan of salted water add the lemon juice and bring to the boil (there should be enough water in the pan to cover three quarters of the height of the artichokes). Before adding the artichokes, trim the stems right back (so that they will sit level on a plate). Add them to the water, stem down. Cover the pan with the lid and boil for 35–40 minutes. After this time, lift them from the pan with a slotted spoon (you should know they are done because the bottom leaves of the artichokes should easily slide off). Tip them carefully into a colander and leave the artichokes to drain upside down.

Preheat the oven to 180C/350F/ Gas 4.

When the artichokes are cool enough to handle, gently prise open the top leaves and scoop out the 'hairy' top part of the heart with a spoon, leaving the heart itself to keep a seal and form your 'bowl'. Fill the cavity of the artichoke with the sauce, wrap in foil and bake in a roasting dish in the centre of the oven for 30 minutes. Remove, open up the top of the foil and spoon in the grated cheese. Leaving the foil still open return them to the oven for a further 10 minutes to melt the cheese.

Remove the foil and serve these stunning artichokes with warm crusty bread.

A EUROPEAN LOVE STORY

Once you're beyond Dover and realised in horror that your jaunt across the cities of Europe is in grave jeopardy because you've forgot to pack your beloved Marmite, just one little sentence should be all you need in the supermarchés and the supermercados of Paris and Barcelona. Aherm...

When pining in Paris:
J'aime Marmite
When desperate in Dusseldorf:
Ich liebe Marmite
When ravenous in Rotterdam:
Ik houd van Marmite
When bereft in Barcelona:
Yo amo Marmite

REPELLENT IN MORE WAYS THAN ONE?

For many years, travellers to the tropics have wondered over the mosquito-repelling properties of their beloved Marmite. The vitamin B complex has been thought by many to repel the airborne bloodsuckers. During the Malaria epidemic of the 1930s in Sri Lanka, tests were carried out on a group of patients. Each patient was given the standard anti-malarial treatment, quinine. They were then given little pill-like globs of Marmite. Starvation amongst the affected was so dramatic that the effect the Marmite had on reviving the patients was wrongly assumed by some to be a sign of its anti-malarial qualities.

From that moment forth, Marmite and its supposed repellent properties has held sway for many!

Marmite Cocktail Sausages

Really fun party food for kids of all ages.

MAKES A BIG BOWLFUL FOR PARTY MUNCHIES

1kg cocktail sausages (or
   chipolatas, halved)
2 tablespoons sesame oil
1 tablespoon Marmite
1 tablespoon lime juice
100ml runny honey
50ml maple syrup

Preheat the oven to 200C/400F/ Gas 6.

Lay the sausages in a shallow roasting tin.

In a bowl, mix together the oil, Marmite, lime juice, honey and syrup and pour all over the sausages. Turn the sausages several times so that they are well coated and then roast in the oven for 30 minutes, turning them a few times halfway through the cooking.

So simple – the job is done and you will have a bowlful of scrummy sausages to hand round with the drinks.

Huntsman's Omelette

If you fall into the group of hunter-gatherers then this omelette will suit you down to the ground. Its basic ingredients mould together to make a great and substantial reward.

SERVES 4

100g fresh white breadcrumbs
pinch ground nutmeg
freshly ground black pepper
75ml double cream
50g butter
1 medium onion, finely diced
60g chestnut mushrooms, sliced
60g chicken liver, finely chopped
2 lambs kidneys, cored and finely
    chopped
2 teaspoons Marmite
vegetable oil for frying
8 free-range eggs, beaten
chopped fresh chives, to serve

Place the fresh breadcrumbs in a bowl, season with nutmeg and pepper and stir in the cream. Leave aside for half and hour so that the breadcrumbs absorb all the seasoned cream.

Melt the butter in a large frying pan and gently fry the onions and mushrooms until soft, then move them to the outside of the pan and add the liver and kidney and cook for 5 minutes. Stir in the Marmite and mix all the lovely ingredients together. Tip them out into a small dish and keep warm.

Add the breadcrumb mixture to the beaten eggs and mix together well. Heat a little vegetable oil in a large frying pan over a medium heat and then carefully wipe out any excess with a pad of kitchen paper. Tip in the egg and breadcrumb mixture and using a fork draw in the sides of the omelette as it cooks for 2 minutes so that you have waves in the middle to give it body. Add in the liver mixture evenly over the egg and then put the pan under a preheated grill for 1 minute to puff up the egg and turn it just golden at the edges. Cut into 4 wedges and serve with the chives scattered over the top.

Quick check-in
China is famous for the only man-made construction that can be seen from outer space, herbal remedies and martial arts.

Departure lounge
The export market for tea is believed to be worth around 50 million US dollars.

Customs clearance
Slurping soup from your spoon is considered good grace. It helps to cool the soup and diffuse flavours.

Nothing (else) to declare?
Pack a knife and fork to save you hours of trying to bluff your way with chopsticks. Better still, just stick to soups and heavy slurping and no-one need ever know your uselessness with the utensils.

On the culinary map
Dim sum is the perfect way to try a little bit of so many good things.

Off the radar
You'll need a mug or two of green tea to hand to wash down the taste of beetles and fish eyes.

Travels around the world
NO.4 China

Singapore Noodles

This is a prime example of a Singapore dish that's quick and simple to make, oozing with classic Oriental flavours married to fine rice noodles.

SERVES 4

250g vermicelli rice noodles
1 tablespoon sesame oil
3 spring onions, finely sliced
100g Chinese leaf, finely sliced
1 teaspoon Madras curry powder
1 teaspoon fresh ginger, peeled
  and finely chopped
200ml chicken stock
1 tablespoon soy sauce
1 teaspoon Marmite
100g small frozen prawns,
  defrosted
100g cooked pork, shredded
120ml Chinese cooking wine or
  dry sherry
150g beansprouts
2 tablespoons fresh coriander,
  chopped

Put the rice noodles into a bowl and cover them with boiling water. Leave for 4 minutes, then drain.

Heat the oil in a wok and fry the spring onions and Chinese leaves for 2–3 minutes. Add the curry powder, ginger, stock, soy and Marmite and keep everything moving for a few minutes before adding the prawns, pork, wine and noodles then shake to combine it well in the wok.

Stir in the beansprouts and coriander and give it all a final toss for 2 minutes then tip into bowls and serve.

Brunch Bruschetta with Tomato and Marmite Scrambled Egg

You just have to try this one, if only to see the rather impressive way that the Marmite marbles into the runny scrambled eggs.

SERVES 2

4 small thick slices rustic bread
2 tablespoons olive oil
2 ripe tomatoes, roughly chopped
few torn basil leaves
salt and pepper
small knob of butter
2 free-range eggs, beaten
1 teaspoon Marmite

Toast both sides of the bread and drizzle each piece with the olive oil.

Mix the roughly chopped tomatoes and basil leaves, season with salt and pepper and pile them onto two of the pieces of toast. Pop them into a warm oven or under a low grill together with the two remaining pieces of toast.

Melt the butter in a small pan, add the eggs, season with a little pepper and keep stirring until you have soft creamy scrambled eggs. Take off the heat and gently swirl in the Marmite to 'marble' the eggs. Pour onto the two other pieces of toast and serve one of each for the perfect brunch.

Calve's Liver with Roasted Red Onions

This is one of the ways Greeks serve their liver, which really appealed to me. Add to this my own little way of roasting onions and you have a delicious combination.

SERVES 4

2 medium red onions, peeled and quartered
2 teaspoons Marmite, warmed
2 tablespoons olive oil
600g calve's liver, thinly sliced
150ml dry white wine
150ml tomato juice
2 cloves
salt and pepper

Preheat the oven to 200C/400F/Gas 6

Place the quartered onions in a roasting tray, brush with the warmed Marmite and drizzle with half of the olive oil. Roast in the oven for 15–20 minutes until the edges of the onions start to crisp. Remove from the oven, turn the oven off and break up the layers of onion with a fork, moving them to one side of the roasting pan. Pop the pan back in the oven to keep warm in the latent heat.

Heat the remaining oil in a frying pan over a medium-high heat and flash-fry the calve's liver for a couple of minutes on each side. You will need to do this in batches and, as each batch is cooked, slide the cooked liver into the roasting pan in the warm oven, retaining the juices in the pan.

To the juices in the pan, add the wine, tomato juice and cloves and bring up to the boil. Add the roasted onions and stir on a high heat until it reduces to a rich sauce and then remove the cloves. Taste and season as required. Divide the liver between four warmed plates and douse with the onion sauce. This is great served with good old English mashed potato to soak up the juices.

Priddy Oggies

An oggie is a West Country name for a pastry or pasty. They were first made, so I understand, at the Miners Arms in Priddy, Somerset. Then, the pasty was made using a lard-based pastry which was first baked and then fried. My modern take – slightly updated – uses puff pastry.

MAKES 6 OGGIES

500g pork fillet, trimmed of any fat
1 tablespoon Marmite
1 free-range egg, beaten
80g Cheddar cheese, grated
2 tablespoons freshly chopped
   parsley
few sage leaves, finely torn
$1/4$ teaspoon cayenne pepper
cornflour, for dusting
500g ready-made puff pastry
12 thin rashers streaky bacon

Cut the pork fillet in half lengthways and beat each half out on a board with a meat hammer or rolling pin until it is really thin (as thick as a 10p coin) and then spread each piece with half the Marmite.

In a bowl combine half the beaten egg with the cheese, parsley, sage and cayenne pepper and mix together well. Spread the mixture evenly over the pork and then roll each piece up as tightly as possible, wrap in clingfilm and chill for 1 hour.

Preheat the oven to 190C/375F/ Gas 5.

Dust a board or clean work surface with a little cornflour and roll out the pastry to the thickness of a pound coin and cut out six square, 15cm in length.

Take the two rolls of pork fillet and cut each into six pieces, wrap each piece with a rasher of bacon and then place two pieces into the centre of each pastry square. Moisten the edges and bring each corner to the centre, pinching the pastry together to form a seal. Place the oggies on a greased baking tray, brush with the remaining egg and cook in the centre of the oven for 25–30 minutes until golden and puffy.

Remove from the oven, allow to cool a little and serve with some delicious Somerset cider.

Malaysian Chicken and Vegetables in Spicy Gravy

Malaysian flavours are always fresh and crisp and this delicious spicy gravy just proves the point.

SERVES 4

50ml peanut or corn oil
2 garlic cloves, finely chopped
1–2 birdseye chillies (according to taste), very finely diced
2 free-range chicken breasts, thinly sliced
1 teaspoon Marmite
1 tablespoon light soy sauce
1 tablespoon palm sugar (or white sugar)
$\frac{1}{2}$ teaspoon ground white pepper
600ml chicken stock
200g small broccoli florets
200g shredded curly kale

Heat the oil in a wok, add the garlic, chilli and chicken and cook gently for two minutes.

Remove from the heat, stir in the Marmite and then add the soy sauce, sugar, pepper and chicken stock. Return to a high heat and boil for 3–5 minutes until the liquid has reduced to a thin gravy. Add the broccoli and curly kale and cook on a medium heat for a further 4–5 minutes, or until the vegetables are tender and the sauce has thickened.

Serve with noodles or rice.

Quick check-in
Perhaps the most famous ancient civilisation of them all, famous too for its pyramids, sphinx and the River Nile.

Departure lounge
Fresh fruit and vegetables, though Indian Jones' pet monkey has probably put us off their dates.

Customs clearance
Eat with your right hand only, always go after second helpings and don't salt your food!

Nothing (else) to declare?
Egypt is a melting pot of wonderful flavours and dishes influenced over the years by neighbours and immigrants.

On the culinary map
Baba ghanoush is a wonderful aubergine dish. And one of the world's best desserts: baklava.

Off the radar
A diet rich in beans, lentils and vegetables, comes with one major wind-assisted downside.

Travels around the world
NO.5 Egypt

Peanut Butter and Marmite French Toast

This must be one of the most popular combinations amongst Marmite lovers: peanut butter, Marmite and gloriously decadent French toast. What could be better?

PER PERSON

1 free-range egg, beaten
2 slices white bread, preferably
   slightly stale
Marmite, for spreading
crunchy peanut butter for
   spreading
1 tablespoon vegetable oil
small knob of unsalted butter

Pour the beaten egg into a flat dish.

Spread one slice of bread with Marmite and one slice of bread with peanut butter – as little or as much as you choose and then sandwich the two together.

Dip the sandwich into the beaten egg on both sides and leave it there while you heat the oil and butter in a frying pan. When the oil is hot, add the sandwich and fry gently for 2–3 minutes on each side until golden and crispy.

Remove from the pan, slice in half and devour.

The Marmite World Chequerboard

Love it or hate it, here is your chance to see Marmite rule the world with this edible chequerboard! Vary the toppings to make this a truly global feast!

SERVES 4–6

6 slices of square-style sliced
  bread
unsalted butter
Marmite
cream cheese for spreading
6 cherry tomatoes
$\frac{1}{4}$ of a cucumber

Lightly toast the bread on both sides and butter it. Spread three slices with Marmite (to the thickness of your choice) and spread the other three with the cream cheese.

Slice the crusts off the toast and cut each slice into six equal-sized squares. Now on a large flat plate or board arrange the squares – alternately Marmite and cream cheese – to form a square chequerboard using all 36 pieces.

Halve the tomatoes and arrange them at random on the squares. Now slice the cucumber lengthways into julienne strips a little thicker than a matchstick and place them in the form of a cross on another random 12 squares.

And there you have an edible chequerboard for kids of all ages! You can vary the toppings to suit whatever your family likes to eat.

Wild Boar Country Curry

If you can't find wild boar then use free-range pork or, better still, rare-breed pork from good butchers or farm shops. This fantastic Thai dish will taste just as good either way. This is curry in a hurry with just a little time devoted to the preparation.

SERVES 4

50ml peanut or corn oil
1 heaped tablespoon red Thai chilli paste
450g boar or pork loin, sliced into strips 3cm long, 2cm wide and 1cm thick
1.25 litres water
200g tin bamboo shoots, drained and diced
150g baby aubergines, quartered (optional)
150g fine green beans
1 teaspoon fresh ginger, peeled and finely diced
2 medium red chillies, quartered lengthways and deseeded
1 tablespoon fish sauce
2 teaspoons Marmite
4 kaffir lime leaves (fresh or dried), torn into small pieces
small handful of torn sweet basil leaves

Heat the oil in a heavy based saucepan and gently fry the chilli paste for three minutes.

Add the pork, stir-fry for three minutes and then remove from the heat and add the remaining ingredients except the basil leaves. Return to the heat, bring up to the boil and simmer for 10 minutes.

Remove from the heat and stir in the basil leaves. This curry is traditionally served with sticky rice but I have even served it with jacket potatoes to soak up the delicious juices.

MARMITE
BY NAME...

The skiiing resort of Åre in Sweden
is home to the Marmite restaurant.
France boasts both La Marmite restaurant,
in Antibes, and La Marmite hotel,
in Estissac. They might be Marmite by
name, but we wonder if they could possibly,
truly be Marmite by nature? A restaurant
that is both thoroughly loved and hated?
A hotel that so distinctively divides opinion
amongst its clientele?

No, there really can be only one Marmite.

MARMITE
BY NATURE...

Around the world – to the huge relief of
ex-pats, travellers and lovers of England's
finest food export – Marmite can be found.
The majority of the Marmite the world
consumes is made at the one factory in
Burton-on-Trent, England. The very same
product is available in Australia and
New Zealand (but sold as 'Our Mate').
Once produced in Burton, Marmite ships
across the world in huge drums and gets
packed into jars at its destination.

Poor imitations will fool no Marmite
afficionado worthy of the name!

Marmite Mushroom and Potato Bake

Mushrooms can be a bit bland but dribble in the Marmite and their flavour bursts into life.

SERVES 4

350ml milk
50ml dry white wine
3 medium potatoes, sliced
25g butter
1 dessertspoon olive oil
2 teaspoons Marmite
300g chestnut mushrooms, sliced
few sprigs fresh thyme, leaves
  only
salt and freshly ground black
  pepper

Preheat the oven to 200C/400F/ Gas 6.

Grease a shallow baking dish. Pour the milk and white wine into a saucepan and bring to the boil. Add the sliced potatoes, season with salt and pepper and simmer gently until tender.

In the meantime heat the butter, oil and Marmite in a frying pan and toss in the mushrooms. Cook for 3–4 minutes turning them all a few times to coat in the delicious juices.

Now simply pour the mushrooms and juices into the potato pan, add the thyme leaves, stir gently and slide the whole lot into the baking dish.

Bake in a hot oven for 40 minutes until crispy and golden on top.

Naan Bread Pizza

Naan bread works really well as a pizza base and you can choose any combination of your favourite toppings... just don't forget the all-essential Marmite.

SERVES 2

2 teaspoons Marmite
2 garlic and coriander naan breads
1 tablespoon tomato purée
4 marinated artichoke hearts
4 chestnut mushrooms, thinly
  sliced
8 cherry tomatoes, halved
freshly ground black pepper
olive oil
100g grated mozzarella cheese
1 tablespoon chopped fresh
  parsley

Preheat the oven to 180C/350F/ Gas 4

Spread the Marmite evenly over the naan breads and then add small dollops of tomato purée all over the top. Cut each artichoke into four and arrange over the naans, then the mushrooms and then the cherry tomatoes. Season with a little freshly ground black pepper and a small drizzle of olive oil.

Sprinkle the grated mozzarella over the top and scatter with the parsley. Put the pizzas onto a baking sheet and cook in the oven for 10 minutes until the edges are just golden and the cheese has melted.

Allow to cool a little, cut in half and serve.

Quick check in
The opera house, kangaroos, koalas and Kylie. Barbecues and Bondi Beach. And curiously quaint phrases such as 'fair dinkum'.

Departure lounge
A major meat exporter – especially beef, but also exotic meats such as wild boar, crocodile and kangaroo.

Customs clearance
Win friends by pitching up at the barbie with a hearty 'G'day', a six-pack and a slab of red meat.

Nothing (else) to declare?
Australians actually throw 'prawns' not 'shrimp' on their barbies. The misleading phrase came into circulation after a 1980s TV advert aired in America.

On the culinary map
The home of the meat pie and, for the sweet-toothed, Tim Tams and Anzac biscuits.

Off the radar
Celebrity TV has broadcast 'bush tucker' food to the world. Still, we think we'll pass on the kangaroo testicles and witchetty grubs.

Travels around the world
NO.6 Australia

Warm Spiced Beef Salad

Warm salads are so in vogue
and and this spiced beef
variation shows just why.

SERVES 4

2 x 225g sirloin steaks
salt and freshly ground pepper,
   to season
1 teaspoon fish sauce
1 teaspoon Marmite added to
100ml hot water
4 spring onions, finely sliced
2 shallots sliced
handful fresh mint leaves
2 tablespoons lime juice
1 teaspoon red chilli paste
1 teaspoon caster sugar
shredded crispy lettuce, to serve

Season the steaks with a little salt,
plenty of fresh pepper and the fish
sauce. Grill or fry the steaks on
both sides to your liking but this
recipe really works best with rare
to medium-rare beef. Slice thinly
and keep warm.

In a small bowl, mix together the
warm Marmite stock with all the
other ingredients except for the
lettuce and a few of the mint
leaves, which you should keep
back to garnish with. Stir in the
beef slices, taste to check the
seasoning and serve just warm
over crispy lettuce with the
remaining mint leaves scattered
over the top.

Thai-Style Oxtail Soup

This northern-Thai twist
is my favourite variation
on a classic European soup.
Both the spices and the Marmite
serve to give it a real kick.

SERVES 4–6

600g oxtail
1.5 litres chicken stock
1 teaspoon soy sauce
2 teaspoons Marmite
freshly ground black pepper
small handful coriander stems,
   finely diced
200g potatoes, peeled and diced
250g tomatoes, quartered
6 small green chillies, deseeded
   and finely diced
100g spring onions, green and
   white parts, diced
1 large clove garlic, crushed
1 teaspoon brown sugar
small handful chopped coriander
   leaves

Preheat the oven to 180C/350F/
Gas 4 and dry roast the oxtail in
a baking tin for 40 minutes.

Remove the skin and discard, then
carefully remove the chunks of
meat from the bones of the oxtail
and set the meat to one side.

Put the stock into a saucepan
and add the soy sauce, Marmite,
pepper and coriander stems.
Bring up to the boil, add the oxtail
meat and simmer for 10 minutes.
Add the potatoes, tomatoes,
chillies, onions, garlic and sugar
and continue cooking over a
medium heat for 15 minutes until
the potato is cooked.

Remove from the heat and serve
in warm bowls scattered with
coriander leaves.

Fried Aubergine with Minted Yoghurt

This is very 'Mediterranean'; in other words, it's a dish that will bring sunshine into your culinary adventures whatever the weather.

SERVES 4

For the minted yoghurt
1 x 250ml tub of Greek-style yoghurt
1 teaspoon ready-made mint sauce
$\frac{1}{2}$ teaspoon caster sugar
1 teaspoon lemon juice
salt and pepper

1 large aubergine
1 teaspoon salt
1 tablespoon Marmite, warmed
olive oil, for frying
3 free-range eggs, beaten
freshly ground black pepper

In a bowl, mix together all the yoghurt ingredients and season with salt and pepper. Chill while you prepare the aubergines.

Cut the aubergine into 1cm slices with the skin still on. Arrange the slices in a colander in a single layer and sprinkle with salt. Leave for 10 minutes and the salt will make the excess liquid come out of the aubergines. Rinse the slices in cold water and pat dry with kitchen paper.

Lay out the aubergine slices and lightly spread both sides with Marmite. Heat some oil in a large frying pan. Season the beaten eggs and pour them onto a flat dish. Dip the slices into the beaten egg and then fry in the oil for 3–4 minutes until golden and crispy on both sides. Keep warm while you fry in a few batches, adding a little more oil as needed.

Serve with dollops of the minted yoghurt as a perfect partner for kebabs or barbecued meat.

Mexican Beanpot with Cornmeal Dumplings

This Mexican dish just bursts with great flavours, cornmeal dumplings and spicy chillies – enough to blow your sombrero off!

SERVES 6

25g butter
1 tablespoon vegetable oil
1 onion, chopped
1 green pepper, deseeded and roughly chopped
1 teaspoon chilli powder
1/2 teaspoon dry mustard
2 large tomatoes, roughly chopped
1 tablespoon Marmite
400ml water
1 x 400g tin black-eyed beans, drained and rinsed
1 x 400g tin red kidney beans, drained and rinsed
100g mature Cheddar, grated
1 tablespoon freshly chopped chives

For the dumplings
200g cornmeal (masa harina – available in good supermarkets)
2 tablespoons plain flour
2 tablespoons vegetable oil
3–4 tablespoons milk
salt and freshly milled black pepper

In a large saucepan melt the butter with the oil and sauté the onion and green pepper until softened. Add the chilli powder and mustard followed by the tomatoes. Spoon in the Marmite and water and stir well, then add both the beans and simmer for 10 minutes. You will need enough gravy remaining with the beans for the dumplings to cook in afterwards without it being too runny, so if the liquid looks too thin, cook a little longer to reduce it. If, however, your beanpot is too dry, add a little more water.

While the beanpot is cooking, make the dumplings. Put the corn meal, flour, a good pinch of salt and a few good grinds of pepper into a bowl, add the oil and mix together gradually adding enough milk to form a soft dough. Drop golf-ball-sized dumplings into the beanpot, cover and simmer for 15 minutes.

When you are ready to serve, lift out the dumplings and keep aside, tip the beans into a large dish, scatter with the cheese and top with the dumplings.

Sprinkle over the chives and serve.

Quick check in
India has so many jewels: the Taj Mahal, the Golden Temple, Bollywood and arguably the most riotous array of colourful spices in the world.

Departure lounge
Curry is the dish which us Brits took from India – to the point where chicken tikka masala is now regarded as Britain's favourite dish.

Customs clearance
Hands are favoured over utensils, though always the right hand. And cleanliness is paramount.

Nothing (else) to declare?
So many people and so many regional variations: India truly is a behometh of the food world.

On the culinary map
From the simplest vegetable curry to the most succulent butter chicken and wonderfully toasted breads: India has many wonders.

Off the radar
With some foods high in fat, very rich and incredibly sweet – not to mention spicy – beware the curse of the old 'Delhi belly'.

Travels around the world
NO.7 India

Butternut Squash with Blue Cheese and Cashews

Close your eyes and wrap your tastebuds around wonderful French blue cheese, cashew nuts and roasted butternut squash. Then add Marmite oil to the fantasy and you will surely be in veggie heaven.

SERVES 4–6

1 butternut squash (about 1kg)
30ml olive oil, warmed and mixed
    with
1 teaspoon Marmite
1 teaspoon fresh thyme leaves
75g unsalted cashew nuts
1 teaspoon chopped fresh chives
100g St Augur (or your favourite
    blue cheese)

Preheat the oven to 200C/400F/ Gas 6

Peel and halve the squash and scoop out the seeds. Cut it into 2.5cm cubes, pop them into a roasting dish and drizzle with the Marmite oil. Add the thyme, toss everything to coat the squash well and roast in the oven for 40 minutes until the squash is tender.

Lift the squash out of the roasting dish to a warm bowl, scatter with the cashews and chives and crumble the blue cheese over the top. Toss everything together gently until the cheese starts to melt and it's ready to serve.

Macaroni and Meat Sauce

This is basically what my Greek friends call *pastitsio* and I have eaten it many times for lunch at a waterside taverna, but never until now with added Marmite, which lends a real richness to the meaty sauce.

SERVES 6–8

50ml vegetable oil
2 large onions, finely chopped
450g minced beef
salt and pepper
2 teaspoons Marmite
1 tin chopped tomatoes
1 tablespoon tomato purée
1 teaspoon dried oregano
500g macaroni
150g grated mild cheese
25g melted butter (for the
   macaroni)
75g butter
50g plain flour
600ml milk, warmed
4 free-range eggs, beaten

You will need a suitable baking dish approximately 30x20cm

Heat the oil in a large frying pan and cook the onions until softened. Add the minced beef, cook until browned and season with salt and pepper. Stir in the Marmite and add the tomatoes, purée and oregano and simmer for 30 minutes. If the meat sauce is too runny, cook for a little longer. If it is too dry, add a splash of water. You are looking for the consistency of Bolognese sauce.

Bring a large pan of salted water to the boil, add the macaroni and boil gently for 8–10 minutes or until it is just al dente. Drain the macaroni and pour half into the baking dish. Sprinkle 50g of the cheese over the pasta and then spread the meat sauce evenly on top. Add the rest of the macaroni, topped with a further 50g of the cheese and finally the melted butter.

Preheat the oven to 180C/350F/ Gas 4.

In a saucepan melt the 75g of butter and add the flour, stirring constantly over the heat until you have a nutty light brown paste. Add the warm milk slowly (to avoid creating lumps), stirring all the time. Add the remaining cheese, leaving a little to sprinkle over the finished dish and a pinch of salt. When the sauce starts to thicken, slowly add the beaten eggs, still stirring well.

Pour the sauce over the pasta and finish with the reserved cheese. Bake in the centre of the oven for 30–40 minutes or until the top is golden. The perfect accompaniment is a crunchy leaf salad.

Brandied Marmite Chicken

To make a great dish you need great ingredients. Here we have aromatic brandy and salty Marmite in a frenzy of taste fusion.

SERVES 4

100g pancetta, diced
1 onion, peeled and roughly
   chopped
1 medium free-range chicken
1 dessertspoon Marmite
50ml brandy

Preheat the oven to 200C/400F/ Gas 6.

Heat a dry frying pan and toss in the pancetta. As soon as the fat starts to run add the onion and fry until golden. Remove the pancetta and onion with a slotted spoon and pop them inside the chicken to give off a delicious flavour when it roasts.

Put the chicken into a roasting pan. Add the Marmite and brandy to the hot juices in the frying pan, let it sizzle for a moment and then pour it all over the chicken.

Put the chicken in the hot oven and roast for one hour or until the juices run clear when pierced with a skewer between the leg and body.

Herb Tagliatelle with Ragù Sauce

Pasta, pasta, pasta – there are one thousand ways of cooking and serving pasta. Try this tagliatelle with the Marmite infusion and you'll never touch the other nine hundred and ninety-nine!

SERVES 4

1 tablespoon olive oil
1 clove garlic, crushed
1 onion, roughly chopped
1 level tablespoon Demerara sugar
100g smoked streaky bacon, diced
450g minced lamb
1 x 400g tin of chopped tomatoes
50ml Marsala wine
100ml water
2 teaspoons Marmite
300g tagliatelle
1 tablespoon chopped fresh parsley
50g Pecorino cheese

Heat the oil in a medium saucepan and add the garlic and onion. Cook gently for five minutes until just golden. Add the sugar and a splash of water and cook for a further five minutes to caramelise the onion. Toss in the bacon and cook until beginning to crisp and then add the minced lamb, breaking it up with a fork while it browns.

Tip in the tomatoes and add the wine, water and Marmite. Bring to the boil and then simmer gently for one hour, adding a little more water if required.

When ready cook the pasta in plenty of boiling salted water until just *al dente*.

Drain and toss with the chopped parsley. Tip the tagliatelle into warm pasta bowls, pour over the ragù sauce and sprinkle with grated Pecorino.

Quick check in
Leaning towers, the Colosseum, expensive shoes and handbags, the Mafia... all found in Italy.

Departure lounge
Italy has given the world the three 'P's: pasta, Parmesan and pizza. Ooh, and ice cream.

Customs clearance
Every Italian firmly believes that their mamma cooks better than anyone else's.

Nothing (else) to declare?
Italians tend to eat full-course meals for lunch and dinner and they enjoy it by eating s-l-o-w-l-y.

On the culinary map
Fresh pasta and pizza, lasagna and bruschetta. Food we know and love, but to try them in Italy is to try them for the first time again.

Off the radar
Sardinia's maggot cheese, Tuscany's pork blood cake and the raw snails of Sicily could be good ones to avoid.

Spicy Meatball and Tomato Soup

This is a Swedish-influenced dish – meatballs, tomatoes, peppers, shallots, herbs and a touch of spice. A warming, savoury blend.

SERVES 4–6

6 large ripe tomatoes
3 red peppers
4 shallots, peeled and quartered
2 tablespoons olive oil
2 teaspoons mixed herbs
250g lean minced beef
salt and freshly ground black
    pepper
2 teaspoons Marmite
dash of Tabasco (more if you are
    brave)
small bunch fresh basil leaves
1 tablespoon tomato purée
300ml vegetable stock
1 teaspoon brown sugar

Preheat the oven to 200C/400F/ Gas 6.

Cut a cross in the top and base of the tomatoes and pop them in a roasting tin with the peppers, shallots, olive oil and herbs. Season with salt and freshly ground black pepper and roast for 20–25 mins until the tomatoes are soft and peeling and the peppers are blistered and blackening.
Lift out the peppers, put them in a bowl, cover with clingfilm and leave for 15 minutes. Leave the tomatoes and shallots to cool in the roasting tin.

Now for the meatballs. Put the beef, Marmite, Tabasco, some torn basil leaves and tomato purée into a food processor, season with black pepper and blitz for a few seconds only. Remove and form into small meatballs, then put them onto a roasting tray and cook for 25 minutes turning them once during cooking.

Peel the peppers, discarding the seeds and pith. Slide the skins off the tomatoes and then add them with the peppers, shallots and any of the roasting tin juices into a blender and blitz until smooth

Transfer the pepper and tomato mixture to a large pan and stir in the vegetable stock and sugar. Taste to check the seasoning and adjust if necessary. Serve in warm soup bowls with the meatballs and a flourish of basil on top.

Za'atar Lamb with Tabbouleh Salad

Traditionally, this Middle-Eastern tabbouleh salad consists of cooked cracked wheat infused with lots of fresh mint and parsley and served with local meat. Here I have added a little sophistication, incoporating the spices and herbs you would find in the local markets.

SERVES 4

For the lamb and marinade
800g lamb fillet
2 tablespoons olive oil
1 dessertspoon Marmite
1 tablespoon sumac (North African spice)
1 tablespoon toasted sesame seeds
1 teaspoon dried thyme leaves
1 teaspoon dried oregano leaves
1 teaspoon sweet paprika

For the tabbouleh
100g cracked wheat
500ml hot vegetable stock
2 tomatoes, finely chopped
50ml extra virgin olive oil
2 heaped tablespoons roughly chopped fresh flat-leaf parsley
1 heaped tablespoon chopped fresh mint
1 medium red onion, finely chopped
2 tablespoons lemon juice
few mint leaves for garnish
salt and pepper

Place the lamb in a large dish and add in all the other lamb marinade ingredients working them well into the meat with your hands. Cover with clingfilm and chill in the fridge for two hours.

Preheat the grill to medium-high and line the grill pan with foil. Grill the lamb for 5–8 minutes on each side, basting occasionally with the remaining marinade until it is dark brown on the outside but still pink in the centre. (Cook for longer if you like your lamb well done.) Remove from the heat and leave to rest somewhere warm for five minutes.

Put the cracked wheat into a bowl. Add the hot stock, leave for five minutes and then, using a fork, loosen the wheat to separate the grains until it is all light and fluffy. Add the remaining tabbouleh ingredients and mix well.
Taste and season with salt and pepper as needed.

Spoon out the tabbouleh into bowls and arrange the lamb in slices on top scattered with a few mint leaves.

FLIGHTS OF FANCY

Marmite has earned its place in our storecupboards. Over the years it has proven its worth, its reliability; that unmistakeably piquant tang and intoxicating whiff will forever be etched on our senses.

But beyond the domestic affection and sentiment that gets heaped upon Marmite, there is also the professional praise that gets bestowed upon this magical dark elixir by some of the country's finest chefs. None finer, nor more succinct, than chef Heston Blementhal, who confesses, 'I'm a Marmite fan.' He uses it in his vegetarian stew which he serves at his three-Michelin-star restaurant, The Fat Duck in Bray.

UNLIKELY
DEPARTURES

To some, the act of eating Marmite in any form whatsoever is something that's all too horrible to contemplate. For others, the humble piece of toast and the odd beef stew represent just the starting point for a whole bastion of experimental ways in which to imbibe and savour their favourite yeast extract. Chef Gary Rhodes, amongst many other creatives and inventors, has dreamed up recipes which include Chocolate Marmite Sauce and Marmite Syrup Coffee Ice Cream.

We say why stop at toast when the world is your oyster?

Mushroom and Hummus Marmite Wrap

The texture of mushrooms and hummus marry together beautifully. Once you add the Marmite you have one of the finest picnic ingredients in the world.

SERVES 2

2 soft flour tortillas
2 teaspoons Marmite
2 tablespoons hummus
1 small jar marinated mushrooms (antipasti)
few leaves crunchy lettuce, shredded
freshly ground black pepper
$\frac{1}{2}$ lemon

Warm the tortillas in the oven for a few minutes to soften them.

Spread each first with the Marmite and then with the hummus. Drain the jar of mushrooms, reserving the oil, and roughly chop the mushrooms. Add them evenly to the tortillas and then scatter with the shredded lettuce. Drizzle with a little of the oil from the mushrooms, season with black pepper and squeeze some lemon juice over it all.

Fold up the bottom third of the wrap and then fold in the two sides. Put a serviette round the bottom it for easy eating on the go.

Rump Steak Kebabs with Horseradish Crème Fraîche

Kebabs, much like the English Breakfast, are found the world over with a local twist. This recipe comes from an Australian chef who taught me to make kangaroo sausages and these kebabs.

MAKES 10 KEBABS

500g beef rump
2 tablespoons Marmite
3 teaspoons freshly grated
 horseradish
1 tablespoon fresh rosemary
 leaves
50ml olive oil
2 tablespoons port
200g crème fraîche
$\frac{1}{2}$ teaspoon Dijon mustard
2 heaped tablespoons chopped
 chives
salt and freshly milled black
 pepper

You will need 10 bamboo skewers, pre-soaked in water a few hours in advance

Cut the beef into 2.5cm cubes. Warm the Marmite a little to loosen it and brush it all over the cubes and spread them out in a shallow dish. Now sprinkle over one teaspoon of the freshly grated horseradish, scatter with the rosemary leaves and drizzle the olive oil over the lot. Turn the meat a few times using a couple of large spoons to really mix in the lovely flavours. Drizzle the port over the top, cover and leave in the fridge for at least 1 hour or even overnight if you wish.

Make the dip by combining the crème fraîche, the remaining two teaspoons of horseradish, the Dijon mustard and chives and season to taste with salt and pepper.

Bring the rump steak back to room temperature and divide the chunks between the 10 skewers. Preheat a grill or griddle to a medium-high heat and then cook the kebabs for 2–3 minutes on each side for rare or longer for medium or well done. Allow them to rest for a few minutes before serving with the creamy, fiery dip. These are great served with potato wedges.

Quick check in
Ahh, the Royal Family, Big Ben, Shakespeare, Stonehenge, cricket, the FA Cup and, of course, Marmite.

Departure lounge
When it comes to condiments, nobody does it better than us Brits: Worcestershire sauce, English mustard, Marmite...

Customs clearance
We're absolute sticklers for table etiquette: now keep those elbows off the table!

Nothing (else) to declare?
Did we mention that the sandwich and the chocolate bar were invented here? England is also the spiritual home of tea.

On the culinary map
Fish and chips, cream teas, roast beef, fry-ups, bangers and mash... comfort food heaven.

Off the radar
We have given the world haggis, deep-fried Mars bars and pickled eggs (and once more not forgetting Marmite, of course).

Boston Baked Beans

This simple but delicious
American classic is from
my first *Marmite Cookbook*.
It's a wonderfully warming dish.

SERVES 10

1kg dried haricot beans,
  soaked overnight
100ml molasses or black treacle
2 tablespoons brown sugar
2 teaspoons dry mustard powder
2 teaspoons Marmite
1 teaspoon freshly ground black
  pepper
1 medium-sized onion, peeled
500g belly of pork with rind

Cover the soaked beans with
fresh water and bring to the boil
skimming off any foam. Reduce
the heat and simmer the beans
until their skins begin to burst.
Drain the beans and reserve the
cooking liquid. Combine the
molasses, brown sugar, mustard
powder, Marmite and pepper
with the cooking liquid.

Heat the oven to 100C/200F/
Gas lowest. Place the onion in
the bottom of a 2-litre ovenproof
casserole and pour the beans on
the top. Score the rind of the pork
and push it down into the beans
rind side up. Pour the seasoned
liquid on top adding enough
boiling water to cover the beans.
Cover the casserole and bake in
the oven for a mere nine hours!

Every hour add boiling water,
if necessary, to keep the beans
covered. Remove the cover for
the last hour of baking so that
the pork browns. Serve with the
pork on top of the beans and
accompany with chunks of the
best sourdough bread available.

Seared Tuna with Stir-fry Greens

There was a time when a wok was considered a cooking pot used only by experts, Today, it's a familiar sight in most family kitchens. It's used here to create a dish that is nothing short of delicious.

SERVES 4

For the tuna
2 teaspoons medium curry powder
1 teaspoon Marmite
1 tablespoon lime juice
1 teaspoon sugar
4 tuna steaks (about 200g each)
1 tablespoon vegetable oil

For the greens
1 tablespoon vegetable oil
1 small clove garlic, finely diced
2 anchovy fillets
200g young spring greens or hispi cabbage, shredded
150g baby leaf spinach, washed
150g mange tout

Mix the curry powder together with the Marmite, lime juice and sugar to make a paste. Using a shallow dish, lay out the four tuna steaks and coat each on both sides with the paste, then set aside.

Heat the oil in a heavy based frying pan and sear the tuna for three minutes on each side so that the centre remains pink – this is important.

Using a wok or large frying pan, heat the oil and add the garlic and anchovies. Fry gently until the anchovies appear dissolved. Turn up to a high heat and add the cabbage, spinach and mange tout, turning and tossing them until they have wilted. Serve topped with the seared tuna.

We hope you enjoyed this cooking experience...

...now go forth and enjoy another!

Acknowledgments

When I wrote the first *Marmite Cookbook* back in 2003 I didn't think for one minute that I would get the chance to delve even deeper into the glories of Marmite. And then my publishers suggested this book – using Marmite as an ingredient of the world; mixing it into some of the classic staple dishes from a host of different countries – and I couldn't have been happier or more inspired!

This time I had a team around me: my chefs at Hartley's Kitchen who have had as much pleasure as I in creating this book, a book which I truly hope you'll enjoy as your very own Marmite Kitchen Companion,

My thanks to my lovely wife, Lynda, whose culinary expertise and complete support makes this book possible. Then to Joss Beechim-Horton for his inspired Marmite creations and to Beth Rowe for all her help and expertise. I would not be forgiven if I didn't give mention to Bentley, our golden Labrador, who loves Marmite even though it makes him rather thirsty.

All this said, without the inspired support of Jon Croft, who publishes my books at Absolute Press, and Matt Inwood, whose creativity never ceases to amaze me, these books would not be possible: huge thanks to you both.

Thank you also to designer Claire Siggery at Absolute Press and to photographer Mike Cooper and food stylist Genevieve Taylor for making the food and these pages look so very wonderful.

Thank you also to the team at Unilever who bless these books (not least for producing these wonderful jars of Marmite!).

Finally, once again to all our friends who have sampled starters, drinks and a raft of Marmite recipes from around the world and who have commented and encouraged from the confines of our supper table throughout: a big thank you.

Its been a wonderful opportunity and an enormous privilege to be allowed to create this Marmite World Cookbook, thank you Marmite: I love you!